Guadalupe Quintanilla

Leader of the
Hispanic Community

GUADALUPE QUINTANILLA

Leader of the
Hispanic Community

Mary Dodson Wade

—*Multicultural Junior Biographies*—

ENSLOW PUBLISHERS, INC.

44 Fadem Road	P.O. Box 38
Box 699	Aldershot
Springfield, NJ 07081	Hants GU12 6BP
U.S.A.	U.K.

Library of Congress Cataloging-in-Publication Data

Wade, Mary Dodson.
    Guadalupe Quintanilla: leader of the hispanic community/
    Mary Dodson Wade.
        p. cm. — (Multicultural junior biographies)
    Includes bibliographical references (p.) and index.
    ISBN 0-89490-637-2
        1. Quintanilla, Guadalupe C.—Juvenile literature. 2. Mexican
    Americans—Biography—Juvenile literature. 3. Mexican American
    women—Biography—Juvenile literature. 4. Educators—United States—
    Biography—Juvenile literature. 5. Spanish language—Study and
    teaching—United States—Juvenile literature. 6. Multicultural
    education—United States—Juvenile literature. [1. Quintanilla,
    Guadalupe C. 2. Educators. 3. Mexican Americans—Biography.
    4. Women—Biography. 5. Multicultural education.] I. Title.
    II. Series.
    E184.M5Q568 1995
    305.48'86872'0092—dc20
    [B]   95-8687
                                                                  CIP
                                                                   AC

Printed in the United States of America

10 9 8 7 6 5 4 3 2 1

Photo Credits: Courtesy of Guadalupe Quintanilla, pp. 12, 17, 19, 26, 31,
38, 40, 42, 48, 51, 55, 57, 64, 69, 72, 74.

Cover Photo: Courtesy of Guadalupe Quintanilla.

CONTENTS

ACKNOWLEDGMENTS

Lupe Quintanilla opened her heart, her office, and her files for my research. A special thanks goes to Martha Ontiveros and to Carlos Gonzalez for their unfailing cheerfulness in ferreting out material and pictures.

DEDICATION

To those at Ripley House, both the givers and the receivers, "for it is in giving that we receive."

THE IMPOSSIBLE
DREAM

Lupe Quintanilla walked out of the office at the college. The woman behind the counter had said, "no." This was the third time someone had said that to Lupe Quintanilla. She was twenty-seven years old, and all she wanted to do was to learn English so she could help her children. But nobody would give her a chance.

She walked slowly down the steps. A young man was standing there. "*¿Quién decide quién puede asistir a la escuela aquí?* (Who says who gets to go to school here?)" she asked.

The young man thought a minute and said, "*Yo creo que es el director.* (I guess it's the registrar.)"

"*¿Dónde está su carro?* (Where is his car?)" Lupe asked. "*Allá* (That one)," he said, pointing to a car in the parking lot.[1]

Lupe headed to the car. She had taken two buses to get to Texas Southmost College. She was not leaving. She had to talk to the person who could let her go to school.

Inside, her feelings were all jumbled. She was angry over being rejected. She was determined to help her children. Still, doubts filled her mind. Could she really do it? What would her family say? And this registrar, would he laugh at her?[2]

Minutes dragged into an hour. She was going to be late getting home. "*¡Ojalá que este señor aparezca!* (I wish this man would show up!)" she thought. Maybe she should leave. She thought about nine-year-old Victor, eight-year-old Mario, and little Martha, who was only six. Her children came first, so she stayed where she was.

All three children were in school now. They had been placed in a group called "Yellow Birds." The teachers said that they were slow learners because they did not know English. It was Lupe's own story all over again.

As a child, she spoke only Spanish. When she came to the United States, she took a test that was written in English. She scored very poorly, and the teachers said that she was retarded.

Determination

Lupe Quintanilla did not want that said about her children. She had made up her mind. If her children needed to know English, she was going to learn English. Her children were going to get out of the Yellow Birds.

Making that decision was easy, but doing it was much harder. First, she thought that she could learn by listening. She asked to sit in a class that trained aides at the hospital, but the person in charge would not let her do that.

Next, she went to the high school. She wanted to sit in an English class, but the school would not accept her.

Now the clerk at the college had turned her away. She could not go to school because she had never been to school.

So here she was, waiting for the registrar. When her feet began to hurt, she perched herself on the hood of the car. That man was not going to leave until he understood why she so badly needed to learn English.

Two hours later the man came out. Lupe

Quintanilla's determination has brought her to where she is today—a speaker, a teacher, an administrator, and a mother.

Quintanilla told him that she wanted to go to college, and he just shook his head. How could she pass college classes? She had never been to high school.

But she insisted, "Just let me try."[3]

The registrar saw Quintanilla's determination and agreed to let her sign up for courses. Lupe Quintanilla had taken her first step on her way to a remarkable career.

DROPPING OUT

María Guadalupe Campos was born in Ojinaga, Chihuahua, Mexico, on October 25, 1937. She was a happy, healthy baby. Sadly, though, when she was eighteen months old, her parents divorced. Isabel Campos left and took her little girl with her. Shortly afterward Lupe's sister Argelia was born.

Bad things began to happen. Lupe became sick and could not walk. Her father carried his daughter to a doctor. The doctor said he should keep the little girl.[1]

Angel Campos raced away with his daughter. He took her to his parents in Nogales, Sonora,

Mexico. Under the loving care of her grandparents, Lupe quickly got better.

She was the light of her grandfather's life. Rosalio Campos had a job inspecting boxcars of the trains that crossed the border into the United States. Lupe often went with him. While he worked, she picked up rocks and interesting things to put in her little box of treasures.

Once she went with him into a boxcar that was filled with tomatoes. Lupe loved tomatoes. Her grandfather did not see the little girl as she ate more and more of them.[2] Before long, she felt very sick.

Helping in the Store

Lupe's grandmother, Guadalupe Campos, ran the grocery store that she and her husband owned. Lupe liked to help in the store. By the time she was five she placed orders for things they sold. Sometimes the person on the phone hung up at the sound of a child's voice. They thought she was playing a joke on them.

Lupe loved to answer the telephone.[3] One day as she ran to pick it up, she slipped and fell into a large tub filled with eggs. Sticky egg yolks and smashed bits of eggshell stuck to her long, curly

Here, Lupe sits with her grandmother who raised her when she was a small child.

hair. It took a lot of washing to get her hair completely clean.

The grandparents adored the little girl. Guadalupe Campos made costumes for Lupe. Rosalio Campos let her keep a pet chicken even though it pecked holes in sacks of flour.[4]

Lupe learned to make cloth dolls. Her grandmother gave her a bag of material to make dresses for them. One day Lupe dug into the bag to find just the right pieces for a dress. When her grandmother picked up the bag, a scorpion fell to the floor. It bit Lupe's grandmother on the toe! For all the times Lupe had put her hand in the bag, she had not been bitten.

She started school in Nogales and quickly learned to read. Soon, however, her schooling ended. Her grandparents sold their store and moved to San Luis San Pedro, Guerrero, to be near their oldest son. He had just become a medical doctor.

In Mexico, doctors pay back the cost of their training by working for the government. It is also the custom for the oldest son to take care of his parents. So Lupe moved with her grandparents to be near her uncle.

Lupe's grandparents were proud of her and took many pictures. They even had a photographer take her picture wearing a cowboy outfit.

Early Learning

The town of San Luis San Pedro had no school, but Lupe loved books.[5] She organized a "school" to teach other girls and boys how to read and do math. Many years later she went back to the little town. "Some of the pupils I had remember[ed] me," she recalls with pleasure.[6]

After three years the family moved again. This time they lived in Matamoros, Tamaulipas. Lupe helped her uncle. By the time she was ten, she was keeping the names of his patients. She knew how to place patients under the x-ray machine. She learned to give shots by practicing on an orange.[7]

In Matamoros Lupe could go to school again. She was placed in the fourth grade because of her age. Reading was her favorite subject. Even today she treasures her Spanish copies of *Pinocchio* and *The Thousand and One Nights*.[8] As top student in the class, she got to carry Mexico's flag in the school parade. She won a string of medals in reading and science. School was a happy place, but her life soon changed.[9]

Rosalio Campos became blind in one eye and wanted to move to a farm. The teacher begged the grandparents not to take Lupe out of school, but it was not possible for her to stay.[10]

A Difficult Move

Life on the farm was different. Sometimes when it rained, they could not get to town for weeks. At times, Lupe's uncle walked through chest-high water to bring them supplies.

They grew cotton and also had lots of chickens. The chickens attracted snakes. Lupe tried to get rid of them with her slingshot, but that did not work very well. She told everyone she wanted a rifle. Her father, who lived across the border in Brownsville, Texas, gave her his .22 caliber rifle. Today she says, "I am a better shot than some police officers."[11] She proved it once in target practice with the Houston, Texas, police chief.

Unable to go to school, Lupe spent long hours reading to her grandfather. Years later she learned that these books were written by famous Spanish authors. At the time she knew them only as wonderful stories.[12] Soon she was able to do speed reading. Her eyes would be at the bottom of the page before she had finished saying the first sentence.

When Lupe's grandfather became totally blind, they had to move into town. Her uncle's house in Matamoros was not large enough for the entire family to live there, so Lupe left her grandparents and came to the United States to live with her father and stepmother.

A Poor Test

As sad as it was to leave her grandparents, life got worse.[13] She had to take an IQ test to get into school. The test was written in English. Lupe did not know any English, and she did not understand the questions. She scored a sixty-four on the test. The teachers placed the bright young girl in the first grade.

At school everyone spoke English, but Lupe did not know what they were saying. Since she was older, the teacher let her put up posters. She also had the job of taking the smaller girls to the bathroom. Doing those things did not require any talking. Lupe knew she was not learning anything. She was terribly embarrassed and unhappy at school.[14]

One afternoon during recess she was sitting by herself. One of the men cutting grass spoke to her. "*Buenas tardes* (Good afternoon)," he said.[15]

Lupe was excited to find someone she could understand and eagerly started speaking Spanish to him.[16] A teacher saw her. She grabbed Lupe by the arm and quickly marched her into the principal's office.

The principal and the teacher treated her as if she had done something terrible. Lupe could not understand the loud, angry voices. Maybe she was not supposed to talk to the young Mexican man. She did not know that students were not allowed to speak Spanish at school.[17]

What she did know was that she would never go there again. "There was no force on earth that was going to make me go back," she said.[18]

She was convinced that she could not learn. And, she was humiliated by the way she had been treated.[19] Lupe Quintanilla dropped out of the first grade at the age of thirteen.

MODEL MOTHER

By the early 1950s, Lupe Campos still had no education. There was not much for a young girl to do in Brownsville, Texas. For a while she did housework to make money, but she still did not learn English.

At sixteen she married Cayetano Quintanilla. He had a good job as a dental technician. She became a housewife, and by age twenty-one she had three children. Victor was born in 1956, Mario in 1957, and Martha in 1959. Lupe Quintanilla's sister Argelia also came to live with the family.

Quintanilla was content.[1] Her family filled her

Lupe is fifteen years old in this picture—just one year younger than she was when she married Cayetano Quintanilla.

life. They lived in a nice house and took interesting vacations during the summer. She was a good cook and loved to sew.

She was proud of her children.[2] In Brownsville, the Charro festival is like Mardi Gras. She made clever costumes for the children to wear in the Charro parades.

Yellow Birds

Quintanilla worried, however, because her boys were not earning good grades in school. When Martha started going to school, Quintanilla helped the Spanish-speaking children in her daughter's class.

One day, she was watching the children as they studied. She noticed that all the children in the Red Birds spoke English. All the Yellow Birds, including her own children, spoke Spanish. She asked the teacher why this was. The teacher told Quintanilla, "Your boys are slow learners. We had to put them in reading groups with children like themselves."[3]

Quintanilla asked the principal about this. He helped her understand. "You speak only Spanish at home. Your boys are confused. They don't know how to function in English."[4]

Those words opened old wounds for Quintanilla. She knew about being thirteen years old and having to sit in the first grade. That was not going to happen to her children! They were going to learn English. They would get out of the Yellow Birds.

To do that, she needed to learn English. She meant to do more than just *speak* English. She wanted to know spelling, grammar, and everything else.[5]

Trying to Learn

First she tried to use her children's books, but that was too slow.[6] Then she thought about the hospital where she was a volunteer. She delivered flowers and mail, and everyone seemed to accept her. When she asked if she could sit in the class where the aides were trained, though, the person in charge turned her away. She was told that she needed a high school diploma. The rejection cut like a knife. Quintanilla thought they respected her as a person. Sadly, they did not care enough to help her learn English. She walked home in the rain with tears streaming down her face.[7]

She did not give up, though. If the hospital

would not help her, maybe the high school would. All she wanted to do was to sit in the back of an English class to listen. The counselor at the school stared at her. "Your records show you to be mentally retarded. I can't recommend your admission."[8]

Still not defeated, Quintanilla went back to her children's school. The principal saw how much she wanted to help her children. He suggested that she try the junior college. He thought they might have a course she could take.[9]

She rode the bus to Texas Southmost College on the other side of town. When she asked about studying English, the clerk said there was no way she could do that. She had never even gone to high school.

Still she did not leave. Somebody was going to teach her English! For two hours she waited by the college registrar's car. When he came out, Quintanilla explained why it was so important for her to learn English. He felt sorry for this determined woman and gave her a special permit to enroll. But he warned, "If you don't make it, don't bother me any more."[10]

Make it she did! The first semester her grades were so good that she was on the dean's list of top students. She continued to do the same thing every semester after that.

Not everything was easy, however. She had to take algebra. She thought algebra was some kind of spaghetti.[11] Later she could laugh at that idea, but not at the time. Algebra made her sick. She came out of class and threw up. Still, she never gave up. The younger students helped her with the pesky algebra.

There were also other things to learn. "The first week of school I didn't drink any Coke™ because I didn't know what button to push on the machine. It was a whole new world," she recalls.[12]

Her family thought she would get tired and quit. She juggled her roles as wife, mother, and student. She got up at 4 A.M. to study. She took the long bus ride to school. At noon she came home to fix her husband's lunch. In the afternoon she returned to class. She then hurried back so she could be home when her children returned from school.

New Goals

Soon she had a new goal—a college degree.[13] She enrolled at Pan American University in

Quintanilla's family has always been the most important part of her life. Concern over her children's need to learn English led her to enroll in college.

Edinburg, Texas, sixty miles away. Two days a week she rode there in a car pool with other students. She did not drop her other college classes either. Three days a week she went to school in Brownsville.

At the end of three years she finished both colleges at the same time. In 1969, she received a Bachelor of Science degree. Her main subject was biology, and she did so well that she graduated *cum laude* (with honor). But something even better happened. Her children began getting better grades. They were proud of their mother.[14]

Lupe Quintanilla had reached one goal. Now, she wanted to learn more. Soon she moved to Houston with her children. Her husband chose not to come.

Again she juggled her schedule. There were classes at the University of Houston, parent conferences, and her children's sports events. Money was tight. She earned small fees by grading exams. She also taught Spanish at the downtown YMCA.

By 1971, she had earned a Master of Arts degree. She studied Spanish and Latin American literature. The University of Houston quickly hired her. Quintanilla was the first Mexican-American woman to teach there.

She was an outstanding teacher and earned the school's Teaching Excellence Award. Not long after that she was put in charge of the Mexican-American Studies program. Soon she headed the Bilingual Education program.

A Long Way from the IQ Test

Honors were not enough. As a teacher, she wanted more education. In 1976, she received the degree of Doctor of Education. Before long she became an administrator and helped run the university. She was the first Hispanic woman to have that position at the University of Houston.

She still teaches courses, but in 1991 she became assistant vice-president for academic affairs. She makes sure that students have finished all their work so they can graduate.

Students come to her office with all types of problems and questions. If they have dropped out of school, they must talk with her before they can enter school again. If they cannot pay the college fees, she is in charge of money that they can use to help them afford school.

Sometimes students want to enroll in the university, but for some reason they do not have the proper credits to do so. Perhaps they have not taken the right courses in high school. As a result, they cannot begin their studies without special permission. Now it is Dr. Guadalupe Quintanilla's turn to say "yes" or "no."

UNDERSTANDING THE LANGUAGE

Soon after coming to Houston, Quintanilla read about a Chicago family that died in a fire. Firemen tried to help them, but they could not understand what they were told to do. Houston has more Hispanics than most other American cities.[1] Quintanilla did not want such a terrible thing to happen where she lived.

In 1977, something else happened. Police arrested a young Hispanic war veteran. He died while in their custody, and a riot broke out.

Quintanilla knew that the police needed to understand the Hispanic community. The Hispanics also needed to understand the police.

She and the director of Ripley House went to see Assistant Police Chief John Bales.

Cross Cultural Communication Program

Ripley House plays a big role in Houston's Hispanic community. As many as three thousand Hispanics come there every day. They take part in tutoring, crafts, exercise, and field trips. They can get help with medical or legal problems. Senior citizens enjoy activities, and meals are sent to elderly people who are unable to leave their homes.[2] It is a place where many good things happen.

Chief Bales realized his officers needed to know Spanish, and Quintanilla knew how to teach them.[3] In his office that day, the three planned the Cross Cultural Communication Program. It would take place at Ripley House.

As part of the program, Quintanilla would teach Spanish to the officers. The Houston Police Department agreed to pay five dollars for each officer who took the course.

The program today is much like it was then. Quintanilla still teaches. For eight weeks, officers come two days a week and spend three hours each session learning "street Spanish." They find out how cultures differ from one another. At the end there is a fiesta where everyone enjoys food and *folklórico* dances.

Before Quintanilla began, she spent time with the police to find out what words the officers needed to know. She read reports of accidents and family arguments. Then she made a list of words and put them into a booklet. She also created a manual for the officers to practice reading and answering questions in Spanish.

The Spanish she uses is not like the Spanish taught in school. Street Spanish is different. For example, in Spanish *cuete* usually means "firecracker." In street Spanish it means "gun." *Fila* means "edge." On the streets it means "knife."[4]

Sometimes street Spanish uses words that are not in the dictionary. *Camión* is the Spanish word for truck. *Cerillo* is the one for a match. In street Spanish the words sound more like English. *Troca* is "truck," *mecha* is "match."[5]

The officers learn to speak politely. They also learn what *not* to say. *Tú madre* means "your mother" in Spanish. It is insulting to say this to a young Hispanic man. Officers learn to say *mamá*, not *madre*.[6]

Members of the Hispanic community and police officers enjoy the fiesta at the end of the course at Ripley House.

A Close Call

The police know they need to be able to speak Spanish. Officer Ted Bell found this out the hard way. He was alone on patrol when his radio reported a robbery at a Mexican restaurant. He quickly drove there. He knew there were four robbers armed with guns and knives.

When he entered the kitchen, he saw a man holding a pistol. "Drop it!" he shouted in English. The man turned toward him. The pistol was still in his hand. Bell kept yelling, "Drop it! Drop it!" The man slowly raised the gun. He emptied out the bullets from the gun and they fell to the floor.

Just then the waitress ran into the kitchen. She said the robbers were gone. Officer Bell had almost shot the cook. "I would have had to live with that all my life," he said.[7]

Officer Bell took the course. In it he learned that he should not even say "drop it" in Spanish. *Tírelo* (drop it) also means "throw it." A person holding a knife might throw it. Instead, officers learn *suéltelo*. This means "let go of it."[8]

An officer who had taken the training had an interesting experience when he yelled, "*Suéltelo!*" The suspect was so startled to hear the officer speak Spanish that he dropped his gun.[9]

Quintanilla (center) helps the police and community members better understand each other.

One time an officer was holding three aliens at gunpoint. One of the aliens began reaching into his pocket. "*Pildoras,*" he said. The officer did not know Spanish and thought the man was reaching for a pistol. Two officers who had come to help explained that the man was reaching for his medicine.[10]

In Quintanilla's programs there is no study of grammar. Instead, officers learn five of the most common verbs. They practice giving fifteen or twenty of the most-used commands. They learn to listen for key words that will help them understand a situation. They also practice speaking clearly because it is very important to be understood.

The list of Spanish words they need is printed in a booklet that will fit in a shirt pocket. The officers take the booklet with them to help fill out reports. The booklet also lists sayings that warn the officers of danger. They learn to recognize "take away his gun" or "jump him from behind" in Spanish.[11]

Quintanilla is a strong believer that "a little bit of Spanish can go a long way in saving lives."[12] At the beginning of the one-hundredth training class she explained, "I care about what happens to you."[13]

Children help in the tutoring of police officers at Ripley House, too. They help by teaching the officers to learn how different people's voices sound.

Community Help

Something else makes her way of teaching different. She uses people in the neighborhood as tutors. They act as victims or witnesses. Police officers use their answers to fill out practice reports.

The tutors can be young or old, male or female. Sometimes even a small child is there. This gives officers practice in hearing all kinds of voices. Emilio Fuentez, an active senior citizen, has been a tutor for Quintanilla almost from the start. "I asked her, 'Can you do something with this old man?'"[14] His wit and quick smile keep things lively.

Young people enjoy being the teacher. They love to play jokes. Once they wrote a sentence on the board. It was a Spanish saying to help them remember vowels. "*El burro sabe más que tú.* (The donkey knows more than you.)" The children doubled up laughing. The officers finally figured it out. They had a big laugh, too.[15]

UNDERSTANDING ACTIONS

The language classes worked well. But that was only part of the program. The officers needed to understand that Hispanics may not act the way people from other cultures do. Then too, there are many Spanish-speaking people. They might be from Mexico, Central or South America, or Spain. They are not all alike.

Understanding Different Cultures

She asked the officers what problems they had. Many said that people didn't give their right names. She knew right away what was wrong.

> You tell me that most Mexicans are liars, but frequently they may be giving you the right answer to a wrong question. You pick up a man whom we'll call Juan Gómez Pérez. You ask him, "What's your name?" He says, "Juan." "No," you say, "your last name." He answers, "Pérez." He's honest. But what you really wanted was his surname, which is Gómez. The computer gives you nothing about a Juan Pérez, whom you know by sight and know has been picked up for driving without a license. "He lied," you say. But he didn't.[1]

In Latin countries people often put their mother's name after their father's name. Their surname (father's name) is the legal one. But officers ask for the last one. To them, that is the mother's name.

Dates can be confusing, too. When they speak or write, Hispanics usually put the day first, then the month, then the year. And they are not avoiding answers when they give times. In English, a watch "runs." In Spanish, it "walks." Time is not exact. An event happened "between three and six o'clock." They do not say, "around 3:30."[2]

It is also important to understand body language. Hispanics are not lying when they do not look at a person when they speak. To them it is a sign of respect.

Some people think that all Mexican men

carry knives. Many do not have any weapons at all, but some do. They may prefer knives because neither person has the advantage. Many think a man is supposed to take care of himself. *Guardaespaldas*, the word for "bodyguard," means "guard your back"—not your body.[3]

Positive Results

The program helped officers learn ways to do their job better. Other good things happened, too. The community and police came to respect one another. Also, police officers became role models for children.

Officer B. W. Burks is an example of how the police try to prevent violence. He had been with the Harris County Sheriff's Department for fifteen years. He asked a child what he thought the officer's best weapon was. The child said it was a gun.

Officer Burks shook his head. He took his pen out of his pocket. "This is my best weapon," he said. "A gun hurts people. It hurts the person who gets shot, and it hurts their family as well. With my pen I can write a report that will keep a bad person in a place where that person cannot hurt someone else."[4]

The program has spread to other states.

Ripley House is where the Cross Cultural Communication Program began. The program has been so effective that businesses and other communities now use similar programs.

In California, Yolanda Castro was nine when she tutored. She said, "It was fun trying to learn Spanish and different words together."[5]

Yolanda's brother Miguel is no longer afraid of law officers. Had he talked to an officer before? "Not really," he said. "But I wouldn't be afraid to now."[6]

There was a fifty-four-year-old man who drove a car for twenty years but never got a driver's license. He learned how to get one and proudly showed it to everyone.[7]

Quintanilla is especially proud of the tutors. By brushing up on their Spanish, many helped themselves as well as the officers. She feels that being able to speak two languages is good for the person and for the community.[8] The program has also brought more Hispanic officers into the police force.

Not everyone was happy at first about Quintanilla's work. Some called her a traitor. There were threatening phone calls. But that did not stop her. She knew things would get better if the two groups understood each other.[9]

Inspiring Others to Learn

The program's success made other groups ask for

training. She now has manuals for firefighters, emergency personnel, airport police, drug enforcement officers, paramedics, and police dispatchers. The manuals have to be updated often. Names for street drugs change almost every week.

The FBI Academy saw the value of the program. "The street language method is the most effective," said Bob Greenwald of the U.S. Department of Justice.[10]

The U.S. Department of Defense asked Quintanilla's help in making films. The subjects are ones she knows well. One was on communication between cultures and the other on Hispanic body language.[11]

She has taken the program all over the United States. It is used in New York, California, Indiana, Illinois, Colorado, Wisconsin, Minnesota, and Michigan. Even security workers at the Pan American Games in Indianapolis, Indiana, were trained this way in 1987.

Chief Bales, now retired, says, "This program has been one of the most successful police-community involvements I have ever seen. It brought the Spanish-speaking community in contact with police officers in a non-threatening

Community members and police officers are reading the pamphlet that Quintanilla developed. The pamphlet helps the officers in their dealings with the Hispanic community.

environment and helped allay [lessen] some of the fears and anxieties expressed by both groups."[12]

Diana Davila is a Texas lawmaker. She began to tutor when she was in junior high school and continued during vacations from her studies at Harvard. She believes in the program. "Dr. Quintanilla had such an innovative program. I grew up down the street from Ripley House, and that served as the beginning of my volunteerism." She loved the role play. It helped her see how people misunderstand each other. "It was a most positive experience. It gave me a sense of accomplishment."[13]

STAY IN SCHOOL

When she was a little girl, Lupe Quintanilla loved school. But she dropped out. Now she spends a lot of her time telling students to stay in school.

States have laws that say children must go to school.[1] But Hispanics are three times more likely to drop out than other students.[2]

Fernando Pérez dropped out when he was fifteen. His grades were poor. His parents did not know how to help him, and teachers were too busy to explain.

For the next two years Pérez hung around Ripley House. Sometimes he played the drums in a band. Mostly, he just loafed. One day, Quintanilla asked him to be a tutor.[3] It changed his life and led to a happy ending. He is married now and hopes to be a police officer.[4]

Too Many Children Quit School

Pérez dropped out because he could not keep up. That happens a lot of the time. There are other reasons students quit. Sometimes they just do not like school, or they may not get along with their teachers. They may believe that they are not treated fairly. They may be embarrassed because they do not have much money.[5]

Another problem is that Hispanic children sometimes are not ready to start school. Then they get farther behind each year. Some high school students are four grades below their age group.[6] Without an education they cannot get good jobs.

Solutions

One cause for a poor start in school is that they do not know English. That happens when no one speaks English at home. This was the reason Quintanilla's children were in the Yellow Birds.

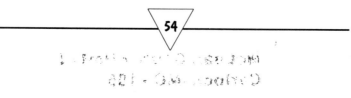

Quintanilla often speaks to people about the reasons why many Hispanic students drop out of school and what can be done to solve this problem.

There is no reason that children need to forget how to speak Spanish. There are successful Hispanics everywhere. They are in business, government, education, and the arts. They all agree that it is important to keep the Spanish language.[7] They also know that they must speak English correctly. Quintanilla believes two languages are better than one. She thinks that people should celebrate being bilingual.[8]

Teachers can help by encouraging students.[9] Quintanilla wants her college students to know how important encouragement is.

Counselors also play a role, either good or bad. Quintanilla's son Mario is an example. He explains, "My counselor must be disappointed. She kept telling me that I was so good with my hands I should become a carpenter."[10] Dr. Mario Quintanilla does use his hands well. He has become a doctor in an emergency room at a Houston hospital.

Children can also help themselves, and Quintanilla explains this when she visits schools. "*Querer es poder* (If you want it, you can do it)," she tells them. She encourages them to set goals. "The more you learn, the faster you get to the goal of what you want to be."[11]

Mario (far right, pictured here with his brother, mother, and sister) was good with his hands when he was young. Because of his skill, his counselor encouraged him to become a carpenter. Instead, he decided to become a doctor.

Sometimes she is not even there when students are inspired by her story. In 1990, ninth grade students in Brownsville, Texas, read an article about her in *Reader's Digest* magazine. They wrote to her. One student, Victor Rosado, talked about his mother. "I'm going to tell her about you. Then I am going to teach her how to talk in English."[12]

Another student, Mary Ramirez, is from a migrant family. Like Quintanilla, she had a hard time with algebra. "For the same reason you accomplished how to learn English, I'm going to try to accomplish algebra."[13]

Quintanilla believes parents should be a part of their children's education. "That's their duty," she says.[14] They can help their children look toward a better future. "The first step is to keep them in school."[15]

A National Interest Develops

Because of her interest in this problem, she worked with actor Edward James Olmos. They created a television program called *Hispanic Dropouts: America's Time Bomb.*[16]

Former President George Bush was also concerned about the number of students dropping out. He wanted to set goals for American school children and asked Quintanilla to advise him about Hispanic students.[17] In 1994, President Bill Clinton signed the Goals 2000 Educate America Act into law.[18]

For her part Quintanilla said, "I was very proud when I got selected for the commission because my life has been dedicated to opening doors for Hispanic students. I have more than textbook information about the issue. I have lived it."[19]

SUCCESS IN BUSINESS

Houston is a very large city. Companies in Houston do business all over the world. People from many countries live in Houston, and there are many Hispanic workers.

People who run the companies know about Quintanilla's work. Some of them had problems of poor understanding among their workers. Besides that, they did lots of business in Latin America. They asked Quintanilla to help them.

One of the companies did not know why it kept losing workers. Quintanilla knew that Hispanics are usually loyal to their jobs. It takes a lot to make them leave. But when they go, they don't say why. She explained that the cause might be that someone had embarrassed them. It is not pleasant when someone says bad things about they way you do your work. She helped the company understand how to treat its workers.[1]

In another case a man went to Mexico City on a business trip. He was ready to sign a million-dollar contract with the company. But he said something wrong. The word he used meant one thing in some Latin American countries, but it had a different meaning in Mexico. He did not know this, and he lost the entire deal.[2]

Helping Different Companies in Different Countries

In order to help a company, Quintanilla has to learn how it works. Every company is different. They have different words they use, and they each have different ways of doing business. Quintanilla finds the right words and teaches the Spanish for them. She finds the problem spots and suggests ways company workers can help their customers.

She writes a manual just as she did for the police. She chooses the words carefully, making sure the Spanish fits the country where the company does business.

Her "shortcut" Spanish works very well. The words fit all kinds of situations. The people who use this Spanish might be oil field workers. They might be people who work at a computer company. She keeps the lessons simple. The workers practice speaking clearly. They must be sure the other person understands them.

Again, learning the language is just part of the course. Quintanilla wants to keep workers from making mistakes. They learn what is important in the place where they will be working. They learn how people react in that country. She stresses being polite. "I always teach at least seven basic courtesy phrases—and words to stay away from."[3]

Business Success in Houston

The city of Houston has a special group that helps companies get business in other countries. This includes Latin America. Councilwoman Eleanor Tinsley worked on that committee. She says that Quintanilla helped them. "She has the sparkle and the knowledge someone needs to talk about cultural differences. She can talk about them from her own experience and she

Quintanilla's experience allows her to speak to all sorts of people about cultural differences—from students to businesses to churches.

can make the listener understand the reasons for those differences—and respect them."[4]

Another success story is Williams Brothers Construction Company. They now have safer, better workers. Ann Garrett explained that the young men had left their families in Central America. They felt comfortable talking with Quintanilla. "You can always get someone to help you through a sticky situation, but Dr. Quintanilla also understands the goals of the company. Every company should have a Lupita."[5]

The program has been so successful that it led to an unusual request. A Catholic bishop in California heard about it. His members were not coming to church, and he asked Quintanilla for help. The people in his church and the bishop now have a better understanding of each other.[6]

José Alvarez was working for the Target™ department stores in Texas when he met Lupe Quintanilla. He knew right away that his company needed to hear what she had to say. The store has workers from many races. Their customers are just as varied. Alvarez wanted all the groups to understand each other. He asked Quintanilla to come to their national meeting to speak to the store managers. She helped build understanding by showing the ways people are different because of their culture.

To Alvarez, Quintanilla is not just someone who helped him with his job. She is a special friend. He explained why. "In a lifetime there is a handful of people who truly touch and change you. I had a coach and a science teacher, and there was a homeroom teacher who told me I could be anything I wanted to be. Lupita has also touched me. She once wrote to me 'Every day has a nice secret.' She has been one of life's secrets for me."[7]

IF I CAN MAKE IT, SO CAN YOU

L upe Quintanilla did not want her children to be called slow learners. To help them, she spent long hours studying English. She became successful, and so did her children.

Magazines and newspapers have told the story of her success. There were articles in both *Reader's Digest* and *The Catholic Digest*.[1] The one in *Reader's Digest* has been translated into thirty-seven languages. *People* magazine also wrote about her.[2] In July 1984 *Ladies' Home Journal* picked one woman from each state for its National Heroine Award. Quintanilla was the one from Texas.[3]

The Houston Post chose her as one of Houston's Top Ten Leaders in 1986.[4] In 1993, *The Houston Chronicle* named her one of Fifty Beautiful Houstonians.[5]

An International Success

Quintanilla has met leaders from all over the world. Former presidents Reagan and Bush asked her to help them. From 1983 to 1986, she worked with President Bush to create laws that would be fair to everyone.[6]

In 1984, Reagan appointed her to be an alternate ambassador to the United Nations.[7] Then, as now, people from all over the world come to New York to work for world peace. Each country has someone to represent it. Quintanilla took the American ambassador's place when she was not there. When Quintanilla's turn came to make a speech, she talked about people understanding each other better. For part of the speech, she spoke in Spanish.

Hispanic groups know how much she has done for them. She has been recognized as Educator of the Year.[8] She helps her students understand the needs of minority children. And she inspires her students:

Former President Reagan appointed Quintanilla as an alternate ambassador to the United Nations. She is pictured giving a speech there—part of which was in Spanish.

> When I came to UH [The University of Houston] to finish my masters, I never dreamed I would be an administrator—or even a teacher. Without my saying it, many times students feel if I made it, so can they.[9]

The schools she attended are aware of what she has done. Pan American University in Edinburg, Texas, chose her as an outstanding graduate. Texas Southmost College in Brownsville, Texas, asked her to speak at the graduation ceremony.

She was elected to both the National Hispanic Hall of Fame and the Hispanic Women's Hall of Fame. In 1992, *Texas Hispanic* magazine listed her as one of twenty-four "Hispanic Women in Power."[10] *La Raza* gave her an award in 1989. They said she helped make things better for Hispanics in the United States.[11] The 1992 *Adelante Mujer Hispana* celebration honored her.[12] She was chosen because she was a role model for women. She helped them to make better lives for themselves.

Women's Rights

Her work with women is not limited to Hispanics. She travels all over America to let women know that they can change their lives. The message is the same one she gives students. But she says it a little differently. "You want, you plan, you persist."[13] She adds "Success is your own definition of what you want to do. . . . You have the character to succeed, the ability to think and to make things happen. Not until you give up have you failed."[14]

In 1991, President Bush sent her to Vienna, Austria. At a conference on women, she made a speech on the importance of getting a good education. Another speech explained how different cultures get along with each other in the United States.[15]

In addition to being a speaker, Quintanilla is a writer. The books and articles connected with her job deal with keeping students in school. But she writes other things, too. She is coauthor of two books in Spanish and has translated books by Spanish authors.[16] It is her goal to complete a book on Hispanic-American women writers. She is also working on a textbook of Hispanic folklore. It will include stories, songs, legends, and riddles written in Spanish.[17]

Quintanilla is grateful for all of the honors that have come to her, but her main interest is in

Former President Bush asked Quintanilla to aid him in making laws that were fair to everyone during the 1980s. He also asked her to go to Vienna, Austria, to speak at a conference for women.

people. She cheered when one of her students was elected to the Houston City Council.[18]

Larry Roser, who is blind, asked her to find someone to read to him. Because she helped him, he sent her a statue that sits on a table in her office. The graceful piece represents freedom of the spirit.

The Importance of Family

If you asked what she was proudest of, though, she would answer quickly, "It is my children." The three were once called slow learners. Now they all have doctorate degrees. It pleases her to say, "When they call my house and ask for Dr. Quintanilla, we have to ask them 'Which one?' because there are four of us."[19]

Victor, the oldest, is a successful lawyer in San Antonio, Texas. He loves sports. Along with his brother and sister, he spends time urging students to stay in school.

Mario works as a doctor in the emergency room at Southeast Memorial Hospital in Houston. He met his goal of getting a black belt in karate at the same time he got his medical degree. Now he is a third degree black belt. His other hobby is astronomy.

Quintanilla is especially proud of her children, pictured here with their mother.
They have all earned doctorate degrees.

Martha is also athletic. She was the first Hispanic cheerleader at the University of Houston. While a student, she was chosen Miss Fiestas Patrias. This festival celebrates Mexico's independence. Martha is proud of her heritage.

As she was growing up, her mother encouraged her to do her best. Today Martha is a lawyer. She is married and lives in Dallas, Texas, where she is an assistant district attorney.

Martha speaks fondly of her mother's support. "She went with me to San Antonio when I took the bar exam. She made sure everything was taken care of so I wouldn't have to worry about it." At times Martha felt that she could not finish. Then she remembered what her mother had done. She knew she could make it too. "Every day I feel so blessed. I see the energy she has, the sincerity in everything she does."[20]

Of her daughter, Lupe Quintanilla says, "I always told her that success is a journey. We're all in the journey."[21]

Mario knows his mother is unique. "I think she is a genius," he says. He is impressed with her speed reading.[22] And he sees her influence in his life. "If we have done well, it is because she has given us the love, the confidence, and the support that enabled us to do well. I feel that God has touched me, and my mother was his hand."[23]

Victor remembers waiting with his mother for the college registrar to come. He thinks that parents should support their children by showing they believe the child can succeed. His mother did that. "She let me know I was capable of more than I thought I was. She told me I could be a lawyer, an astronaut, a pilot, or whatever I wanted to be."[24]

Lupe Quintanilla made her own success happen. She is modest about it, though. "I feel complimented because I represent the university, my community, middle-aged women struggling to develop. But most importantly, I represent opportunity in this country."[25]

Were there hard times? Of course, but she was not defeated by them. "If I'm not successful in something I want to do, I'm successful in finding out why I wasn't."[26]

The guide for her life has been a verse from a poem by Amado Nervo.[27] She translates it in this way:

When I got to the end of my long journey
through life,
I discovered that I have always been the
architect of my own destiny.
If I planted roses along the way, I harvested roses.
And I need not look at the thorns, but look at the
roses.

CHRONOLOGY

1937— María Guadalupe Campos is born on October 25 in Ojinaga, Chihuahua, Mexico.

1950— She arrives in Brownsville, Texas, unable to speak English.

1953— She marries Cayetano Quintanilla.

1957— Guadalupe Quintanilla gives birth to her first son, Victor.

1959— Quintanilla has second son, Mario.

1969— Quintanilla earns a Bachelor of Science degree from Pan American University.

1971— Quintanilla earns a Master of Arts degree from the University of Houston.

1972— Quintanilla begins her teaching career at the University of Houston.

1973— Quintanilla receives Teaching Excellence Award, University of Houston.

1976— Quintanilla earns a Doctor of Education degree from the University of Houston.

1977— Quintanilla co-authors *El espíritu siempre eterno del Mexico-Americano* and *Español: Lo esencial para el bilingüe.*

1978— Quintanilla translates *The Trap and Other Writings*, by Lucy Garibay. She also develops and implements the Cross-Cultural Communication program for the Houston Police.

1983— Quintanilla is appointed by the president as co-chairperson of the National Institute of Justice.

1984— Quintanilla receives a presidential appointment to the United Nations as Alternate Delegate.

1986— Quintanilla works with Edward James Olmos on the television program "Hispanic Dropouts: America's Time Bomb".

1987— Quintanilla is elected to the National Hispanic Hall of Fame.

1989— Quintanilla receives the *La Raza* Award.

1990— A Texas exhibit, "Women in History," includes Quintanilla.

1991— Quintanilla becomes the Assistant Vice President for Academic Affairs at the University of Houston. She is also appointed by the president to the World Conference on International Issues and Women's Affairs in Vienna, Austria.

1995— Quintanilla translates the picture book *I'm Going to Texas/Yo Voy a Tejas*, by Mary Dodson Wade.

CHAPTER NOTES

Chapter 1

1. Personal interview with Guadalupe Quintanilla, March 24, 1994.

2. Ibid.

3. Ibid.

Chapter 2

1. Personal interview with Guadalupe Quintanilla, March 26, 1994.

2. Ibid.

3. Ibid.

4. Personal interview with Guadalupe Quintanilla, March 24, 1994.

5. Elva Salazar, "Designer of Her Destiny," *Rio*, Fall 1986, p. 17.

6. Ibid.

7. Personal interview with Guadalupe Quintanilla, March 24, 1994.

8. Ibid.

9. Ibid.

10. Personal interview with Guadalupe Quintanilla, March 27, 1994.

11. Ibid.

12. Personal interview with Guadalupe Quintanilla, March 24, 1994.

13. Personal interview with Guadalupe Quintanilla, March 31, 1994.

14. Personal interview with Guadalupe Quintanilla, March 24, 1994.

15. Salazar, p. 18.

16. Ibid.

17. Ibid.

18. "'Birds' of Education Changed Woman's Life," *Abilene Reporter News*, October 22, 1984.

19. Personal interview with Guadalupe Quintanilla, March 31, 1994.

Chapter 3

1. Joseph P. Blank, "The Triumph of Guadalupe Quintanilla," *Reader's Digest*, June 1984, p. 78

2. Elva Salazar, "Designer of Her Destiny," *Río*, Fall 1986, p. 18.

3. Blank, p. 77.

4. Ibid.

5. Blank, p. 78.

6. Personal interview with Guadalupe Quintanilla, March 26, 1994.

7. Telephone interview with Guadalupe Quintanilla, April 11, 1994.

8. Blank, p. 78.

9. Ibid.

10. Barbara Karkabi, "I Have Lived It," *Houston Chronicle*, January 14, 1992, p. 4D.

11. Gary Taylor, "The Lady & The Cops," *Dallas Times Herald*, Westward Section, April 10, 1983, p. 15.

12. Ibid.

13. Salazar, p. 18.

14. Blank, p. 79.

Chapter 4

1. Joseph P. Blank, "The Triumph of Guadalupe Quintanilla," *Reader's Digest*, June 1984, p. 80.

2. Personal interview with Lupe Garza, March 24, 1994; personal interview with Margie Peña, March 31, 1994.

3. Telephone interview with John Bales, April 4, 1994.

4. Personal interview with Guadalupe Quintanilla, March 24, 1994.

5. Guadalupe Quintanilla, "Speaking Their Language: Houston Fire Fighters Learn to Work with Hispanic Citizens," *The International Fire Chief*, October 1982, pp. 25–26.

6. Guadalupe Quintanilla, "Cross-cultural Communication: An Ongoing Challenge," *FBI Law Enforcement Bulletin*, undated, p. 5.

7. Gary Taylor, "The Lady & the Cops," *Dallas Times Herald*, Westward Section, April 10, 1983, p. 14.

8. Personal interview with Robert Jones, March 24, 1994.

9. Personal interview with Guadalupe Quintanilla, March 24, 1994.

10. Guadalupe C. Quintanilla and Harry D. Caldwell, "The Houston Police Department's Hispanic Culture/Language Program," *The Police Chief*, September 1979, p. 57.

11. Guadalupe C. Quintanilla, *Conversational Spanish for Law Enforcement Officers*, University of Houston, 1993, pp. 76–77.

12. "Police Learn Spanish to Bridge Cultures," *Houston Metropolitan Magazine*, November 1982, p. 55

13. Cross Cultural Communication Program training session, April 19, 1994.

14. Personal interview with Emilio Fuentez, March 31, 1994.

15. Cross Cultural Communication Program training session, March 24, 1994.

Chapter 5

1. Joseph R. Blank, "The Triumph of Guadalupe Quintanilla," *Reader's Digest*, June 1984, p. 80.

2. Guadalupe Quintanilla, "Cross-cultural Communication: An Ongoing Challenge," *FBI Law Enforcement Bulletin*, undated, p. 4.

3. Ibid., p. 5.

4. Personal interview with B. W. Burks, March 24, 1994.

5. Aurelio De La Torre, "Hispanic Cultural Awareness," *Inland Empire Hispanic News*, 1989.

6. Ibid.

7. Quintanilla, p. 6.

8. Personal interview with Guadalupe Quintanilla, March 24, 1994.

9. Blank, pp. 80–81.

10. Gary Taylor, "The Lady & The Cops," *Dallas Times Herald*, Westward Section, April 10, 1983, p. 16.

11. *Curriculum Vitae: Guadalupe C. Quintanilla.*

12. Telephone interview with John Bales, April 4, 1994.

13. Telephone interview with Diana Davila, March 24, 1994.

Chapter 6

1. *Information Please Almanac,* New York: Houghton Mifflin Co., 1994, p. 863.

2. Statistical Abstract of the United States, 1992, U.S. Department of Commerce, p. 160.

3. Guadalupe Quintanilla, "Dropping Out of School: An Epidemic in Search of a Cure," *Vista,* September 7, 1986, p. 13.

4. Personal interview with Guadalupe Quintanilla, April 19, 1994.

5. Quintanilla, p. 13.

6. Ibid.

7. "100 Influentials," *Hispanic Business,* November 1989, p. 26.

8. Personal interview with Guadalupe Quintanilla, March 24, 1994.

9. Quintanilla, p. 13.

10. Ibid.

11. Veronica Flores, "Love for Children Drives Brownsville Native," *The Brownsville Herald,* October 18, 1988.

12. Letter, Victor Rosado to Guadalupe Quintanilla, October 1990.

13. Letter, Mary Ramirez to Guadalupe Quintanilla, October 1990.

14. Flores.

15. Ibid.

16. *De Colores Productions, Hispanic Dropouts: America's Time Bomb*, television program aired September 17, 1986.

17. "A Progress Report to the Secretary of Education from the President's Advisory Commission on Educational Excellence for Hispanic Americans, October 12, 1992," U.S. Department of Education, p. 4–3.

18. "Education Act Signed," *The Houston Post*, April 1, 1994, p. A-11.

19. Barbara Karkabi, "I Have Lived It," *Houston Chronicle*, January 14, 1992, p. 1D.

Chapter 7

1. Victoria McNamara, "Closing Language Gap Closes Deals," *The Houston Post*, as printed in *The Brownsville Herald*, February 11, 1993.

2. Ibid.

3. Ibid.

4. Ibid.

5. Ibid.

6. Personal interview with Guadalupe Quintanilla, March 31, 1994.

7. Telephone interview with José Alvarez, April 11, 1994.

Chapter 8

1. Joseph P. Blank, "The Triumph of Guadalupe Quintanilla," *Reader's Digest*, June 1984, pp. 77–81.; Gary Taylor, "Guadalupe Tried, Tried Again," *Catholic Digest*, September 1983, pp. 31–35.

2. Kent Demaret, "Top," *People*, October 10, 1983, pp. 69–70.

3. "Fifty American Heroines," *Ladies' Home Journal*, July 1984, p. 143.

4. "Women on the Move; Houston's Top 10 Leaders for '86," *The Houston Post*, November 16, 1986, p. 1G.

5. "50 Beautiful Houstonians," *The Houston Chronicle*, July 4, 1993.

6. *Curriculum Vitae: Guadalupe C. Quintanilla.*

7. Ibid.

8. Ibid.

9. Molly Ancelin, "Architect of Her Own

Destiny: Guadalupe Quintanilla," *Houston Digest,* June 25, 1984, p. 18.

10. "Hispanic Women in Power," *Texas Hispanics,* April/May 1992, p. 44.

11. "Coalition: Partnership for Progress," National Council of *La Raza*; annual conference, July 19, 1989.

12. "Adelante Mujer Hispana," *El Sol, USA,* undated.

13. Veronica Flores, "One-time Dropout Tells Youth to Finish School," *The Brownsville Herald,* December 9, 1993.

14. Dolores Hope, "Successful Woman Beats Odds," *Garden City Telegram,* May 3, 1990.

15. *Curriculum Vitae: Guadalupe C. Quintanilla.*

16. Ibid.

17. Personal interview with Guadalupe Quintanilla, April 19, 1994.

18. Barbara Karkabi, "I Have Lived It," *Houston Chronicle,* January 14, 1992. p. 1D.

19. Juan Espinosa, "Hard Experiences Lead to Helping People Understand," *The Pueblo Chieftain,* April 10, 1993.

20. Telephone interview with Martha Quintanilla-Hollowell, April 4, 1994.

21. Chris Kelly, "Legacy," *Houston Metropolitan* Magazine, May 1992, p. 46.

22. Telephone interview with Mario Quintanilla, April 22, 1994.

23. Blank, p. 81.

24. Telephone interview with Victor Quintanilla, May 4, 1994.

25. Ancelin, p.18.

26. Ibid.

27. Ancelin, p. 18; confirmed in personal interview with Guadalupe Quintanilla, April 19, 1994.

GLOSSARY

administrator—A person who manages affairs, usually for a school, business, or government.

algebra—A form of mathematics which uses letters to represent numbers.

aliens—Persons who are not citizens of the country where they live.

bilingual—The ability to speak more than one language.

cum laude—Latin phrase meaning "with honor," showing that a person earned very high grades.

custody—To be responsible for taking care of something.

grammar—The correct use of words and punctuation in a language.

humiliate—To embarrass or make someone feel ashamed.

innovative—To be new, different, unusual, or have a better way.

IQ test—A series of questions used to test the intelligence of a person.

Mardi Gras—A festival celebrated with carnivals and parades.

registrar—A person who enrolls students in a college.

scorpion—A relative of spiders that has a poisonous sting that is very painful and sometimes causes death.

surname—A person's legal name or family name.

x-ray machine—A machine that takes pictures of the inside of the body.

BIBLIOGRAPHY

"Adelante Mujer Hispana." *El Sol, USA*, undated.

Alvarez, José. "Diversity." *Target Assets Protection Newsletter*, Vol. 13, 2nd quarter, 1993.

Ancelin, Molly. "Architect of her own Destiny: Guadalupe Quintanilla." *Houston Digest*, June 25, 1984.

"'Birds' of Education Changed Woman's Life." *Abilene Reporter News*, October 22, 1984.

Blair, Gene G., and Sam L. Slick. "Survival Spanish Is Needed in Training for Police." *Police Chief*, January 1990.

Blank, Joseph P. "The Triumph of Guadalupe Quintanilla." *Reader's Digest*, June 1984.

"Coalitions: Partnerships for Progress." Program. National Council of *La Raza*. 1989 Annual Conference, July 19, 1989.

Coleman, Fran. "Dr. Guadalupe C. Quintanilla."

Curriculum Vitae: Guadalupe C. Quintanilla.

De La Torre, Aurelio W. "Hispanic 'Cultural Awareness'." *Inland Empire Hispanic News,* August 30, 1989.

Demaret, Kent. "Top," *People,* October 10, 1983.

"A Dropout Who Achieved—Dr. Lupe Quintanilla." *Young Hispanic Women, Leaders for the 90's,* developed by Eva Ross. Ysleta Independent School District, Spring 1989.

Espinosa, Juan. "Diverse Group Gathers to Help Pueblo Policemen Learn Spanish." Pueblo, Colo.: *The Pueblo Chieftain,* June 4, 1993.

———. "Hard Experiences Lead to Helping People Understand." Pueblo, Colo.: *The Pueblo Chieftain,* April 10, 1993.

———. "Police Get Most 'Bang for Buck' in Hispanic Culture Program." Pueblo, Colo.: *The Pueblo Chieftain,* April 6, 1993.

"Fifty American Heroines." *Ladies' Home Journal*, July 1984.

"50 Beautiful Houstonians." *The Houston Chronicle*, July 4, 1993.

Flores, Veronica. "Love for Children Drives Brownsville Native." Brownsville, Tex.: *The Brownsville Herald*, October 18, 1988.

———. "One-time Dropout Tells Youth to Finish School." Brownsville, Tex.: *The Brownsville Herald*, December 9, 1993.

"Former School Drop-out to Speak at Hispanic Banquet." Western Michigan University: *Western News*, September 19, 1991.

Gutierrez, Joe. "S.B. Kids Share Culture with Elders; Latino Students Teach Police in Communication Program." *The San Bernadino County Sun*, August 17, 1989.

"Hispanic Women in Power." *Texas Hispanics*, April/May 1992.

Hope, Dolores. "Successful Woman Beats Odds." Kansas: *Garden City Telegram*, May 3, 1990.

Karkabi, Barbara. "'I Have Lived It'." *Houston Chronicle*, January 14, 1992.

Kelly, Chris. "Legacy." *Houston Metropolitan Magazine*, May 1992.

Kreneck, Thomas H. *Del Pueblo; A Pictorial History of Houston's Hispanic Community*. Houston: Houston International University, 1989.

McNamara, Victoria. "Closing Language Gap Closes Deals." *The Houston Post*, as printed in *The Brownsville Herald*, February 11, 1993.

Morgan, Patti Jones. "I Can't Read." *Houston Metropolitan Magazine*, August 1989.

Ocañas, Hilbert, S. "El Triúnfo de Guadalupe 'Lupita' Quintanilla," *Primero: A Magazine for Houston Hispanics*, August/September 1989.

"100 Influentials." *Hispanic Business*, November 1989.

"Outstanding American Women of Mexican Descent." Teacher's guide developed by Olga de Leon at the Division of Extension, University of Texas, Austin, Tex., undated.

"Police Learn Spanish to Bridge Cultures." *Houston Metropolitan Magazine*, November 1982.

"Profile: Guadalupe Quintanilla." *Perspectives*. University of Houston, March 1985.

"Pueblo Police Start Cross-Cultural Program." Pueblo, Colo.: *The Pueblo Ledger*, March 31, 1993.

Quintanilla, Guadalupe. "Bilingualism." In *Preparing Teachers for Bilingual Education*. Washington D.C.: University Press of America, 1979.

———. "Cross-cultural communication: an Ongoing Challenge." *FBI Law Enforcement Bulletin*, undated.

———. "Dropping Out of School: An Epidemic in Search of a Cure." *Vista*, September 7, 1986.

———. "Non-Traditional Program for Police Officers." *Texas Police Journal*, June 1979.

———. "Speaking Their Language: Houston Fire Fighters Learn to Work with the Hispanic Citizenry." *The International Fire Chief*, October 1984.

Quintanilla, Guadalupe C., and Harry D. Caldwell. "The Houston Police Department's Hispanic Culture/Language Program." *The Police Chief*, September 1979.

Reagan, Belinda. "Quintanilla Tapped for Federal Post." University of Houston: *The Daily Cougar*, June 29, 1983.

Rodriguez, Lori. "Police Officers, Spanish Community Getting Acquainted in Language Classes." *The Houston Chronicle*, September 17, 1982.

Salazar, Elva. "Designer of Her Destiny." *Rio*, Fall 1986.

Samet, Mary. "Lupe: Perseverance Personified," In *Concepts/1986, Golden Key National Honor Society,* 1986.

Sanchez, Tom. "Plan, Persist and Succeed." Laredo, Tex.: *Laredo Morning Times,* March 20, 1988.

"Second Law Enforcement Cross Cultural Seminar Held in High Desert." *Inland Empire Hispanic News,* December 13, 1989.

"Seminar to Challenge Women to Make Choices." *Amarillo Sunday News-Globe,* October 25, 1987.

Taylor, Gary. "Guadalupe Tried, Tried Again." *Catholic Digest,* September 1983.

———. "The Lady & The Cops." *Dallas Times Herald* Westward Section, April 10, 1983.

Texas Police Association 81st Annual Conference and Seminar Program. June 15–18, 1980.

"Women on the Move; Houston's Top 10 Leaders in '86," *The Houston Post*, November 16, 1986.

Yanke, Jewel. "Former Dropout to Keynote Area Displaced Homemakers." *Amarillo Reporter*, April 21, 1989.

INDEX

ABOUT THE AUTHOR

Mary Dodson Wade grew up loving books. That is why she got a master's degree in library science and spent twenty-five years as an elementary librarian. Mrs Wade lives with her husband in Texas. When not ferretting out information in some library, she finds it absolutely necessary to visit her daughter in Boston and her son in Honolulu.